MESSIOLOGY

THE MYSTERY OF
HOW GOD WORKS
EVEN WHEN IT DOESN'T
MAKE SENSE TO US

D0391760

MOODY PUBLISHERS

CHICAGO

Interior Design: Ragont Design
Cover Design: Erik M. Peterson
Cover Image: Cover image of metal wire cube copyright © 2010 by
        Kurt Drubbel / iStock (14129172). All rights reserved.

ISBN: 978-0-8024-1485-4

We hope you enjoy this book from Moody Publishers. Our goal is to provide high-quality, thought-provoking books and products that connect truth to your real needs and challenges. For more information on other books and products written and produced from a biblical perspective, go to www.moodypublishers.com or write to:

Moody Publishers
820 N. LaSalle Boulevard
Chicago, IL 60610

3 5 7 9 10 8 6 4 2

Printed in the United States of America

CONTENTS

FOREWORD

George Verwer has nearly seen it all—everything that can and does go wrong among Christians. His practical wisdom reflects experience with God's people in innumerable settings, including churches, denominations, and mission agencies.

Yet, Verwer has, for over fifty years, been a grace-oriented reconciler, a friend of sinners, and a lighthouse of practical wisdom. This book is just that—not a thriller, nor a devotional, but a handbook of applied biblical insights, born of experience, to help the reader avoid getting wrecked on the shoals of life. There is applicable wisdom to imbibe in every chapter for the servant of God who is determined to please the Lord, and pass it on to those in their midst.

I have been able to "press on" through fifty-three years of ministry, reconciled to those I've offended and able to bolster many others, largely due to having been graced to hear and take Verwer's exhortations seriously. Read on, and "do likewise."

DR. GREG LIVINGSTONE, founder, Frontiers

ACKNOWLEDGMENTS

I want to thank all those who helped make this book a reality, but even more I want to acknowledge the hundreds of people who have had major spiritual input (often via books or tapes) into my life, and especially my spiritual father, Billy Graham, and the second most influential Christian leader in my life, Dr. Oswald J. Smith. I also want to thank the Lord for my sister Barbara, my parents, and my wife Drena and our family.

INTRODUCTION

My passion for books—which goes back to my conversion—has always been for other people's books. I've spent a lifetime publishing and distributing books by great men and women of the faith, and even as I look back at my own books I think one of their best features is the way I introduce my readers to so many other authors. You'll find many more of them recommended in the following pages.

One thing I do enjoy about writing is getting to go through the letters readers send to me. One of my first books, *Come! Live! Die!* (now titled *Hunger for Reality*) brought me over 25,000 personal letters. It's been a great encouragement, and I can only give thanks to the Lord.

Another of my books, *Drops from a Leaking Tap*, features a chapter on the biggest change in both my life and the history of Operation Mobilization (OM). It was the embracing of social concern and action as a vital part of our ministry. In this new book I want to elaborate more on that development, with all its challenges and complexity, and on how easy it is to get into difficulty. I have a great passion to pass to the next generation all I have learned from the Lord and His people.

I have made mistakes in my life and ministry, and I know that many others have as well. I hope that by sharing some of my own pitfalls others may learn by observation to avoid serious damage to themselves and to the body of Christ.

When I was eighteen and heading west to the Grand Canyon, I stumbled upon my life verse while reading the book of Acts:

> *However, I consider my life worth nothing to me; my only aim is to finish the race and complete the task the Lord Jesus has given me—the task of testifying to the good news of God's grace.*
>
> Acts 20:24

Now, looking back after fifty-eight years in Christ, I can say that this has been the case on more or less a daily basis. My prayer in whatever years remain is that it will continue to be my reality. Can you feel the passion of this verse? Can you read it and make it your goal and aim in life as well? If so, I think you will find this book helpful in more ways than one.

A few days ago I took Drena, my wife, to a wonderful concert at the Royal Albert Hall in London. Even now as I type, I am enjoying classical piano music by Tchaikovsky, Mozart, and Beethoven. I trust that at least some of what I write, especially about forgiveness and grace, will be like music to your spiritual ears. That it will bring into balance the challenges of radical discipleship and grace, as expressed in books like *Radical* by David Platt, and *Grace Awakening* by Charles Swindoll. And I also want to add a plea for global missions and evangelism at any cost—that all the people of the world might have the gospel, and that the church would be among all peoples.

Chapter 1

MESSIOLOGY

When I first wrote *Out of the Comfort Zone*, one of my greatest hopes was to see a reawakening of grace, especially among those involved in global missions.

Again and again we hear of tensions among those working to reach the world with the gospel. Many local churches go through very heavy and complex divisions. This is why I believe we desperately need a theology of "messiology."

Put simply, *messiology* is the idea that God in His patience, mercy, and passion to bring men and women to Himself often does great things in the midst of a mess. That is not an excuse for sin or failure; every Christian should strive to avoid making a mess. But it's the other side of the coin.

It's God's way of working in spite of (actually, by means of!) the messes we make to bring about His plan and purposes. I sometimes refer to this as "radical grace." Large portions of Acts and the majority of the epistles demonstrate this.

Throughout the Scriptures, we see God working through all kinds of messy situations. For years I have quoted a personal proverb: "Where two or three are gathered together in His Name, sooner or later there will be a mess." Almost always the congregation laughs. I then ask, "How many have experienced that?" and most hands go up.

Gordon MacDonald's book *Rebuilding Your Broken World*, along with many other great books, has helped me develop this theology of *messiology*. It has helped me understand God and His work more than almost anything else.

Over the course of fifty-seven years in over ninety countries and thousands of churches and other organizations, I have often observed some kind of mess within them. Sometimes clear sin is involved that needs to be repented of. Other times it is just silly stuff. I have said, and I feel it strongly, that no matter how filled we are with the Holy Spirit, we are still human. Our humanness has its beautiful side and its messy side.

I admire many Christian leaders, and try to have a grace-awakened attitude toward all of them, but many of us (including me) do ridiculous things and say even more ridiculous things. Yet as I have observed more carefully, I have seen God working in the midst of it. I have even seen many people used of God who were clearly living in sin at the same time. We have all heard of pastors being used of God—their churches growing with people being saved and discipled—and yet it is later discovered that they were living in adultery and unfaithfulness all that time. These are married pastors with children. Of course, after some time, their sin usually finds them out and the consequences fall like dominoes: they are fired, disqualified from church leadership, sometimes divorced, and so on. But years later, I sometimes meet with the person and his new wife and discover them being used in ministry. If I wrote a book about that, I could give hundreds of similar examples. This is messiology in action!

When it comes to messiology, some other key words are *mystery* and *mercy*. The last verses of Romans 11 have helped me again and again:

> *Oh, the depth of the riches both of the wisdom and knowledge of God! How unsearchable are His judgments and unfathomable His ways!* (v. 33 NASB; see also vv. 34–36)

The hardest thing for some people—especially leaders— to understand is that God can work in a mighty way through someone with wrong theology. How can this be? I meet people who are upset with certain televangelists. Many people tell me that they will not even watch them. I agree with these criticisms. Things I have seen and heard on "Christian" TV make me weep, especially the deceptive fund-raising tricks that some TV preachers employ. But do not be surprised when you get to heaven and meet hundreds of thousands who came to Christ through these ministries. Do we need more of the apostle Paul's attitude as shown in Philippians 1:15–18? It is both clear and hard to accept that God uses ministries and people that we may want nothing to do with. He uses preachers and ministries that I would not even send a dollar to. We want to explain these things and try to fit them in our box, but they will not fit! The answer—*messiology*.

Another area where things get very messy is in the whole area of finance and funding for mission fields, people, and projects. Periodic stories about the misuse of funds in missions prevent some people from sending any money at all to worthy causes. I am convinced that history will show that the generosity and risk of supporting a project (like a school) thousands of miles away have been major factors in taking the gospel forward and establishing His church.

Some people will not support a new school or other similar projects if they do not see how it can be self-supporting right away. But this thinking is misguided because, in places like India, self-supporting schools have been popular for many years, and as a result there are very few good schools for the poor (generally Dalits or tribal people), but thousands of schools available for those who can pay. In the complex situation of extreme poverty, we must expect to put a lot of money in before a school can sustain itself. In the case of some schools it may not be until a couple of decades—when people who graduate from these schools have jobs—that they can be self-sustaining. It's hard to even imagine what we are up against in India with almost 300 million locked into the extreme poverty of untouchability. These exceptional situations, and there are many around the world, call for exceptional generosity.

That doesn't mean we should not exercise discernment and research with regard to all that we give. We need the right people on the field to handle the finance, and the project itself is the most important factor of all. But those who think that they wasted money on a project that went totally wrong may discover many great results of their giving when they get to heaven.

In all of this we need to have wisdom, common sense, and especially beware of what I call *destructive idealism*— the perfectionistic expectations many of us have, which can cause discouragement, disunity, and confusion. A little more wisdom, patience, and humility would go a long way in taking us into greater reality and victory.

Chapter 2

FIRE EXTINGUISHERS, BOOKS, AND PROVERBS

One of my many failures during the early days of our work was to not be in the hospital in Leigh, Lancashire, when our daughter Christa was born. I was coming in from meetings overseas and did not quite make the mega event. Since today, as I write, it is Christa's birthday, I dedicate this chapter to her.

We named her after Christa Fisher from what was then East Germany. Christa had come to Jesus in the early days of our ministry in Madrid, where we lived when we first came to Europe in the fall of 1960. That was right before Ben, our first son, was born.

This story begins even before that, during the summer of 1957, when three of us friends were planning a trip to preach the gospel and distribute literature in Mexico. We didn't go until mid-July since Dale Rhoton was studying at Wheaton Summer School, so Walter Borchard, who had been my college roommate at Maryville, and I were selling Christian books door to door near my home in northeast New Jersey. I had already been selling fire extinguishers in that area for a number of years and that business had been successful. I would light a fire in a pan in front of someone's house and then, while they watched in amazement, put it out with this little Presto Fire Extinguisher. I soon recruited others to sell them and made a handsome profit. My boss was a man from Manhattan and, at sixteen, I felt quite special going to meet with him there. He was so happy about my sales volume that he made me the exclusive agent for Bergen County and I officially registered my company as Bergen County Sales Co. All was going well until Jesus came into my life and led me into the "Eternal Fire Extinguisher" business! So, while Dale was at Wheaton Summer School, Walter and I were selling Christian books in New Jersey to earn money for our trip.

I especially remember one particular lady in North Haledon. After buying a lot of books, which made me happy, she told me something I've never forgotten. I think she could tell I was big on zeal but weak on wisdom, so she challenged me to read the "wisdom" book of Proverbs in the Old Testament. "A proverb a day will keep the devil away," she said. Then she opened her Bible to Proverbs and showed me how there were thirty-one chapters, one for every day in the month, and said I should read a chapter every day. I'd been slowly making my way through the Old Testament and hadn't gotten to Proverbs yet, but that night I did what she said, and I've been in Proverbs ever since. Little did I know what God had in store for me, and how much the wisdom and exhortations of this book would help me in my forty-six-year pilgrimage as leader of Operation Mobilization.

What are some of the themes that hit me the hardest? Here are four highlights.

Victory over lust. There are hundreds of Bible verses about sex, and some of them seem pretty wild and out of the box! For example:

May your fountain be blessed,
    and may you rejoice in the wife of your youth.
A loving doe, a graceful deer—
    may her breasts satisfy you always,
    may you ever be intoxicated with her love.

Proverbs 5:18–19

That's good advice! And to make sure it sinks in, consider the consequences of not taking it to heart:

All at once he followed her [the adulteress]
    like an ox going to the slaughter,
    like a deer stepping into a noose . . .
Many are the victims she has brought down;
    her slain are a mighty throng.
Her house is a highway to the grave,
    leading down to the chambers of death.
                   Proverbs 7:22, 26–27

As a young Christian, so hungry for God and so radically committed to Jesus and His Word, I had no idea I would battle with this all my life. Again and again I would read Proverbs 5, 6, and 7, and that gave me the strength to defeat this ongoing challenge.

The chapter about this in my book *Drops from a Leaking Tap*, was one of the hardest things I had ever written when it first came out as a magazine article. Thankfully, many people were helped by it, which led us to become one of the major distributors of books on this subject in many languages around the world.

Sins of the tongue show up again and again in Proverbs. Just try these verses on for size!

A gentle answer turns away wrath,
but a harsh word stirs up anger.
The tongue of the wise adorns knowledge,
but the mouth of the fool gushes folly.
The eyes of the LORD are everywhere,
keeping watch on the wicked and the good.
The soothing tongue is a tree of life,
but a perverse tongue crushes the spirit.
Proverbs 15:1–4

Even fools are thought wise if they keep silent,
and discerning if they hold their tongues.
Proverbs 17:28

Those who guard their mouths and their tongues
keep themselves from calamity.
Proverbs 21:23

I discovered the hard way how easy it is to hurt people with unkind words. In my case, the one I hurt the most was my own wife! It was through reading books like *Calvary*

Road by Roy Hession, and *Humility* by Andrew Murray, that I learned how to humble myself, repent, and apologize. Thankfully, due to God's work of grace in my life, the "revolution of love" that I've written about has been a growing reality in me.

Pride is the thing that keeps us from realizing how our words affect other people, so I have declared war on all forms of pride. Verses like Galatians 2:20 have become part of my spiritual DNA, and the lack of emphasis today on this truth in many churches and among some leaders is one of the present-day weaknesses that concern me the most—and often leads to "messy" situations.

Billy Graham was a huge help to me with his powerful messages on the seven deadly sins. I got them in printed form to read and distribute. These messages hit me so hard I can tell you exactly when and where I read them: 8 Tasso Road, Fulham, London. It was February, 1962, and we lived there in a one-bedroom flat that Hoise Birks talks about in his autobiography, *A New Man*. We had just arrived in the UK and the name Operation Mobilization was being used for the very first time.

Laziness. I remember at an OM conference in India back around 1967 that I asked people to share their biggest struggle. To my surprise, many of them said laziness. I think this became even a bigger problem there because of the extreme heat, and I experienced some of it myself. My early reading of Proverbs back in New Jersey had warned me about lack of discipline and laziness in its many forms.

Diligent hands will rule,
but laziness ends in forced labor.
The lazy do not roast any game,
but the diligent feed on the riches of the hunt.
                    Proverbs 12:24, 27

One who is slack in his work
is brother to one who destroys.
                    Proverbs 18:9

Laziness brings on deep sleep,
and the shiftless go hungry.
A sluggard buries his hand in the dish;
he will not even bring it back to his mouth!
                    Proverbs 19:15, 24

The sluggard says, "There's a lion outside!
I'll be killed in the public square!"
Do you see someone skilled in their work?

They will serve before kings;
they will not serve before officials of low rank.
Proverbs 22:13, 29

I was blessed in my childhood to have a very hard-working father who taught me well in that biblical ethic, so I had to learn the hard way how to be patient with those who did not have that same work ethic. Sadly, my strong emphasis on work and discipline would lead some people into pretension. People would behave one way when no one was watching, but quite differently when someone from the team was watching. Later they would feel condemned, which could lead to all kinds of spiritual and emotional confusion. This is why, again and again, our whole movement—and especially my own life—was rescued by "radical grace."

Anger. I started getting into fights at a young age, once even with a girl who sort of beat me up. I remember forming a little gang on my street in Wyckoff, New Jersey, when I must have been around twelve. We fought with acorns that fell off the trees. Albert led the other gang and we were enemies. One day I wrote the most popular swear words of our day with black paint on the side of his big white house. Shirley, the girl across the street, must have seen me and told my dad. He really did not appreciate this early outbreak of art and I had to go and paint over it. It seems funny in retrospect, but the truth is that anger could have destroyed my life.

I remember visiting a man in prison who had killed another man. He went to his girlfriend's house by surprise and found another man with her. In a burst of anger he killed him on the spot. When I met him he had found forgiveness in Jesus and was pressing on in prison sharing his faith.

Though I've had a high level of victory in this important area, I've also had my failures, which to this day I remember well. Impatience, which often accompanies anger, has been one of my weaknesses. But I have never given up the fight, and when I fail, I turn to the reality of these verses from 1 John:

If we claim to be without sin, we deceive ourselves and the truth is not in us. If we confess our sins, he is faithful and just and will forgive us our sins and purify us from all unrighteousness. If we claim we have not sinned, we make him out to be a liar and his word is not in us.

1 John 1:8–10

My dear children, I write this to you so that you will not sin. But if anybody does sin, we have an advocate with the Father—Jesus Christ, the Righteous One. He is the

27

atoning sacrifice for our sins, and not only for ours but also for the sins of the whole world.

1 John 2:1–2

I feel so strongly about this that I urge people to never marry someone who does not have victory over anger. If the person has had major anger problems in the past there is a high chance that after marriage it will flare up again and there will be physical violence. Domestic violence, even among those who claim to follow the Lord, is one of the sins the church has been very gifted at covering up—especially if it's a pastor, elder, or worship leader. If you are failing in this area you need to get help. Just reading Proverbs will not be enough. You need help—God's help—which will always include repentance and walking in the light.

This is the message we have heard from him and declare to you: God is light; in him there is no darkness at all. If we claim to have fellowship with him and yet walk in the darkness, we lie and do not live out the truth. But if we walk in the light, as he is in the light, we have fellowship with one another, and the blood of Jesus, his Son, purifies us from all sin.

1 John 1:5–7

There are so many vital subjects in the book of Proverbs and I can't address them all here. My main reason for mentioning these few is to get you reading it regularly and dealing by faith with every issue the Lord speaks to you about. I also encourage you to read and practice 2 Timothy 2:2 by sharing what you have learned with others, who can then pass it on to others.

And the things you have heard me say in the presence of many witnesses entrust to reliable people who will also be qualified to teach others.

2 Timothy 2:2

Chapter 3

UNITY IN THE MIDST OF DIVERSITY

I am in Germany at an unusual place as I type this chapter—the Mother House of the Deaconess Movement of Aidlingen. I have been coming here for about forty years. In a few weeks they will again put up a huge tent on their property and have one of the largest youth events in the nation with more than 8,000 coming from all over to hear the Word of God and great Christian music.

I remember speaking here some years ago, and it is always amazing to see God working in the hearts of so many young people. These dear sisters take vows of chastity and some think of them as Protestant nuns (though they are actually members of the Lutheran Church here in Germany).

I consider it a great privilege to have some of these sisters in Jesus as close friends. This is one of my favorite places in the world to slow my pace and give myself to prayer, writing, and walking in the great forest surrounding the grounds. I also share from the Word of God with them and have great fellowship around the wonderful meals they provide. Their deep love for Jesus and His Word and desire for world missions are very evident.

After sixty years of ministry in close to a hundred nations, I have come across a sprawling diversity of movements, churches, and people. Just on our ship *Logos Hope* alone, you will find forty different nationalities. No wonder the prayer nights are so interesting!

Wisley Garden, a botanical garden with thousands of varieties of flowers just outside London near Heathrow Airport, is another one of my favorite places. My close friend Danny Smith, who came to Jesus when I first met him in Calcutta almost fifty years ago, lives near there, and we sometimes go for walks among the flowers. The breathtaking variety of this vast garden reminds me of the church across the world with its more than 40,000 denominations and movements—a number that's increasing every year!

I have heard leaders I respect speak about this colossal explosion of movements and denominations in a negative way. I, too, was once of that mindset. But seeing the diversity of people the Lord used in the Bible and the variety of the stars and galaxies in almost every area of creation, I realize it's largely a wonderful and positive thing. Truly we are one church spiritually, united in Christ. But in an earthly sense, why are we not all united as one church in the same denomination? I think the answer is easy. That's not God's way of building His kingdom on Earth. So within the stream of orthodox, biblical Christianity, we should celebrate this great diversity. Even in the midst of the messiness caused by our sin—divisions, discord, disunity, strife—God is at work.

There are many secondary issues that have caused churches and denominations to split, but the great global split has been between those who believe the Bible is truly God's Word and those who don't. Many years ago, the word "fundamentalist" was coined to distinguish those who believe the Bible is the Word of God from those who do not; those who do not were often called "liberals" (not in the political sense). In more recent decades, "evangelical" came to describe those who hold to the biblical faith but who generally do not want the label "fundamentalist," which has been connected with hyper-legalism and judgmentalism, and even compared to Islamic fundamentalism. That's why thousands of churches and hundreds of movements associate themselves with the

WEA (World Evangelical Alliance) or the national counter-part in their own nation. The WEA helped to cultivate in me a greater respect for the wonderfully different ways God was working in so many denominations and movements.

We must face the fact that so much of church growth, social concern, and service takes place within the context of the local church. Yes, God uses interdenominational movements as well. But we should eschew an either/or mentality and real-ize that God works in different people in different ways.

Of course, the more we can have times of praise, fellow-ship, worship, and evangelism, as the body of Christ united together, the better. Certainly without sincere love for one another we only hinder ourselves and our own church or movement.

God works through culture, language, people, situations, and all kinds of circumstances. Most churches or movements over the last two thousand years were started by a vision-ary leader. Up until Martin Luther in the sixteenth century, there were only a few major divisions, but at the same time the Catholic Church learned how to channel diversity into differ-ent orders, so we saw a huge range of them—like the Jesuits, Franciscans, and Sisters of Mary. There isn't enough space for me to write about the great errors that crept into that church in those days, many of which still remain today. It was truly a "messy" time in church history. But would any of us dare to say God was not doing anything in the midst of it?

Many today are especially critical of all our different churches and denominations, but I recommend they go to Wisley Garden. As fallen human beings, everything we touch—yes, even the church—will be fraught with sin, weakness, faults, and failure. But God is at work even in our fallenness and humanness. The great mystery is how our great God keeps working and doing wonderful things in the midst of it all.

This does not mean we should lay aside our battle for greater holiness or forget that Satan is a roaring lion seeking those he can devour—even by appearing as an angel of light. The reality of the spiritual warfare outlined in Ephesians 6 is very real. We must not make excuses for sin and folly, but always repent and try to make things right, by God's grace.

Moreover, we are well aware that some churches and denominations are spiritually dead. Heresy and false teachings have arisen, smothering the gospel and replacing the truth with error. We must all fight the good fight—pursuing sanctification by the Spirit, seeking unity in the church, and guarding against falsehood. Yet, don't be surprised if God remains steadily at work in the midst of the mess, bringing lost souls to Christ and glory to His Name!

Chapter 4

COMPLEXITY, COMMUNICATION, AND MESSIOLOGY

I am very aware as I write this book that many might read it and find it quite over the top or confusing. But sooner or later, they will meet people and churches and Christian groups that are over the top and confusing—and much worse. The bottom line of this book is the greatness and mercy of God because of what Jesus Christ has done for us on the cross. For more on this foundational truth, I recommend John Stott's *Basic Christianity*.

Maybe you're among those who are confused or even discouraged by what you have seen or experienced in the church, or some other Christian ministry. If so, please read on. I want to share from my heart some of the areas where I have struggled with disappointment, discouragement, and even doubt and unbelief.

For a long time I have listened to Christians and Christian leaders who are critical of other Christians, churches, or organizations. This includes people I respect and love and from whom I have learned. My problem is not only the lack of concern and love I see, but that so often they don't have the facts right or take things out of context. I wish that fifty years ago we had books like *Leading with Love* or *If You Bite and Devour One Another* by Alex Strauch, whom I have come to appreciate so much, or *Calvary Road* by Roy Hession and *Love Is the Answer* by Theodore Epp. Books like these help us cultivate the Christlike love and understanding that are often missing when we rush to criticize or condemn our brothers and sisters in Christ.

I myself have fallen into this trap. As a young leader I was sometimes one of the most critical of other leaders, churches, or organizations. I slowly learned to be more positive, but only when I developed a different view of the way God works—and who He works with—was I able to see positive things being done through people, churches, or organizations that I thought were in error.

In *The Grace and Truth Paradox*, Randy Alcorn shows us that we can have both a strong commitment to truth and also love and grace. We should be much slower to criticize, especially when we really don't have the whole story.

However, we can't forsake or neglect our strong commitment to the truth in the name of "grace." True grace stands not in conflict but in harmony with truth. Scripture commands us to defend the faith. We could all be helped in this area by a fresh look at the second and third epistles of John.

In this chapter I want to share some of the areas that have caused me so much confusion and struggle.

Literature: I first started selling books and leaflets door to door after I had been a Christian for two years. Before going to Mexico in the summer of 1957, a magazine called *Floodtide* came into my hands, and then I became involved with the Pocket Testament League. The value of the ministry of the printed word, even before I was converted, was clear to me. I was blessed reading Christian books and leaflets and wanted, with total sincerity, to bless others. Looking back at a lifetime with books I can shout, "God uses books!" But what you might be surprised to also hear me say is that God can even use poor books! I discovered that books I did not like and would not sell because of their extreme or untruthful teachings were also used of God to help bring people to Christ as Savior.

How do you handle someone being helped and blessed through a book that you believe contains harmful or deceptive teaching? How do you explain God using books in a mighty way when the author has now fallen into sin? Even more complex is that books written by great men and women of God often disagree—maybe even on important issues.

How do we decide what to believe? It sometimes seems easier for young believers to decide what they believe on quite complex issues and doctrines. I will not be around, but I wonder how my grandson will be at my age. God in His mercy and mystery and grace often does great things in the midst of the mess—this is messiology.

Television/Internet: If we think the world of Christian literature is complex, then try television and now YouTube, the Internet, Facebook, and all that's coming down the road. The world of technology is mind-blowing. Research shows that TV preachers, whom some of us can hardly stand to watch or listen to, have helped not thousands, but tens of thousands come to Christ all over the world. In response to that, some people immediately say, "Well, most of them must be false conversions." But the truth is, I have met many of these people all over the world over the past fifty years and they seem like authentic believers. Many of them have been used of God not only to see others come to Christ, but to start thousands of churches. Remember, we are still in the midst of the greatest harvest of people coming to the Lord that the world has ever know. I have heard critics say that many, or most, of those who make decisions in those kinds of meetings are not really saved; they're mostly false conversions as someone converted through the most highly criticized preacher in my lifetime, Billy Graham, I would beg to differ.

We say that people are saved by grace as they put their faith in the Lord Jesus Christ, but seem to indicate in our behavior that keeping all the rules and regulations is really where it's at in terms of us knowing who is a true Christian. Please read *Extreme Righteousness* by Tom Hovestol and you will discover, as I did, how strong believers in truth can so easily develop a Pharisee streak. Charles Swindoll's *Grace Awakening*, especially the chapter "Graciously Disagreeing and Pressing On," was such a huge help to me in combatting these Pharisaic tendencies.

Music: God has used and is using all kinds of music to help people worship and come to Jesus. This has been another saga of complexity over the last fifty years. It's almost a miracle that from the beginning I was in favor of what

41

eventually became "contemporary music." The New Testament does not say that much about music, and the Old Testament has quite a wide range of both music and dance. It is astounding how much controversy came from this. Tens of thousands of churches around the world have split over the traditional versus contemporary music controversy. On the one side, some even said that drums are from Satan (I have a copy of a booklet that says that!). Back in the old days I listened to tapes and read books by some people who condemned much of the music that I saw God using in such a mighty way. This could have discouraged me immensely if I had not developed a different view of God, His love, and the way He works. He must have a great sense of humor as He watches the way His children behave.

If you think this is a small issue or that it has gone away, a closer look at what's going on in the wider church might change your mind. Some have even lost their faith and walked away from the Christian church because of what they saw in terms of extreme statements and harshness over the music issue. In the end, it seems that the new and contemporary music has won the day, but it is not all over yet. Even the volume at which music is played has presented a new set of problems (I do admit I carry earplugs almost everywhere). Quite a few notable musicians falling into immorality or divorce have made it an even messier scene. Then musicians speaking strongly against other musicians did not help. Some people seem to write off the whole Christian music industry with stories about greed, pride, and immorality. But in the midst of the mess, God was doing such a great work and so many were coming to know the Lord.

Those of us who read widely will become over-exposed to negative reports and Christian horror stories. We should beware of trying to prove a point by pointing to negative stories, since there is almost always more to the story, and it doesn't consider the full scope of what God can do in the midst of the mess and all our humanness. We all need to memorize Romans 8:28: "And we know that in all things God works for the good of those who love him, who have been called according to his purpose."

Where is God in all of this? I say right in the middle! He is loving, forgiving, saving, and using all kinds of, what the Bible calls, "clay pots" to accomplish His purposes. We don't have to leave a church because it prefers traditional hymns or contemporary worship songs; we can stop condemning those who take a different road when it comes to issues like this. I say to my peers in the 60s and 70s club: "What is more important, that we enjoy the music or that more of the next generation come to know and worship Jesus?" Do we have any idea of what God has done through churches like Hillsong and their music? Multiply this by 10,000 and we might get some idea of what our God is doing around the world through all kinds of music and people. Get some earplugs and press on.

Politics: Right wing, left wing, no wings. In the United States right now this is an area of great controversy and division among God's people and it's getting worse by the day. I strongly believe that God can work through a divided and broken church (speaking of the whole body of Christ). After all, that's all He's ever had to work with!

That, however, is never an excuse for a lack of love, or any other sin. Much of the problem is linked with the fact that some people believe in the "Christian nation" theory and others don't. I don't believe in the "Christian nation" theory, but I love those who do. All nations in all times have operated in the midst of overwhelming evil. Those who believe that is all going to change in the future are deceived, but I love them as well.

I majored in history before transferring to Moody Bible Institute in Chicago and have studied history ever since. We can learn so much from history. Reading different viewpoints is hard, and finding out what actually happened is even harder, so all history students should at least be humble and maybe a little less dogmatic. Should Christians engage in hateful language and circulate hateful emails? I don't think so, but if they do, somehow our mighty God still loves them and may use them more than I would ever want. So please don't get discouraged by the mess in this area or in the government, but try to focus on God and what He is doing in the midst of it. We have many thousands of years of history to show what God can do in the midst of a mess.

We must still operate as the salt and light in our world, and I don't mean that Christians should not get into politics or that there is no room for patriotism. God works within our culture and these things are an important part of our culture. The more true Christian values we can see in society, including our own community, the better, but we shouldn't force them and legislate them. We must not mix government with the church. Too many are fighting the dark instead of spreading the light. It's a losing battle and not worth all the effort. Let's get our priorities right. More than that, let's respect that God will lead different people and different churches in different ways. Why not go the extra mile in respecting God's guidance in other people? On many related issues we all are never going to agree, but I hope we can agree that our God can do great things in all kinds of situations—including those we would run away from.

Chapter 5

THE CHURCH, MISSIONS, AND HOLLYWOOD

In the previous chapters I touched on a few areas where things seem quite complex and messy. I am sure you don't want to read much more along those lines, but allow me to let you in on the many areas I have been reading and talking to people about for half a century or so. I believe understanding this will help us all become more grace awakened, big hearted, and forgiving. I believe you will have greater wisdom and discernment to handle tough situations—especially if you are a leader.

Church Governance: I never could have believed as a young Christian how many different ways there are to lead a church and how the Lord seems to bless so many different methods. Often those who have a particular method believe in it very strongly and if you are among those I am not asking you to change, but I would encourage you to maybe be a bit less dogmatic that your way of doing it is the only way. Even changing our vernacular a bit to something like "one of the ways" would be so much more sensible than saying "this is the only way."

We now have team-led churches (sometimes called elder-led) that go back to the Brethren Movement, which was such a dynamic movement in its day and in some cases still is today. Dale Rhoton, who went to Mexico on that very first trip and who I met at Maryville College, became part of that movement and wrote a booklet that this was the New Testament way. I was only beginning to understand this unique movement, having first worshiped among this group in Mexico City. William MacDonald, who at that time was president of Emmaus Bible College in Chicago, was becoming a friend and supporter. His book *True Discipleship* became a great influence in our movement. There were many factors leading me to be baptized by immersion by Dale at Bethany Chapel in Wheaton. However, at that stage in my life I was already very interdenominational as Moody Bible Institute helped me down that road.

And then I married a Baptist! Dale and a few others were commended from their assembly to work with OM, and we considered that a great answer to prayer. Little did we know that some years later I would end up starting the work in the UK where the Brethren Movement was born and it is still going strong. Historically, a number of our leaders, including our first UK director, Keith Beckwith, and later Peter Maiden, who became my associate director and then successor, were linked with them. The Brethren Movement has had many splits; almost every individual assembly has had one, but God keeps working and it is still a relatively healthy global movement. Some now have pastors who try to lead while still being a team player. Others are horrified by the idea of having a pastor and this has caused more splits. Let's be honest, in God's mysterious way of working, splits and division are one of the ways the church grows. That is not to excuse any sin or misbehavior. As always, the concept of God working in the midst of the mess stares us in the face.

There is not space to go into all the different ways that churches are led. To the surprise of many of us, our work in India, totally under the leadership of Indians, chose to go down a road that seems to combine the Brethren, Baptists,

Methodists, and the Anglicans with a charismatic streak. The Good Shepherd Churches are one of the greatest fruits of our entire history, but we had to let them find their own way, and my change of view on how our God works has helped me understand it more than I can express. You can be sure I am a raving fan and strong supporter of what's going on, but that does not mean I agree with it all or even understand it all. Whenever there are large numbers coming to Christ at once, it is not just a mess but a hyper-mega mess. That's why we should pray and support more than ever that great work and other similar works. Through this rapid growth we have learned that *mistakes cost us*. We also learned more about how the devil and his helpers can use gossip to try to destroy a work. We must all be more positive about the many ways that God works in such a variety of churches with different styles of leadership.

Hollywood and Christian Movies: I loved good films and some bad ones as a young kid, so it was quite a shock as a young believer to be told that films and the cinema are all from the devil. While it is no longer the case, back in those days at Moody I had to sign a paper saying that I would not go to films. I was so strong for Jesus and world missions that in a sense I did not want to take any chances and on many issues I went along with the order of the day. Only later did I realize a lot of it was legalism and I was soon in its clutches. One thing is for sure, we have hundreds of years proving that God can work in the midst of a legalistic environment. But I believe the Bible teaches there is a better way. This is linked with culture and the amazing way God seems to be able to break into almost any cultural situation. When a Texan gets saved, he stays a Texan. That may irritate our Christian folks from Boston, but it's no big deal with the living God. A lot of misunderstanding between states, nations, and cities could be resolved if we were more God-centered and understood His amazing ways better.

Our movement ran parallel with the Christian Film Movement under the leadership of people like Ken Anderson and many others. Even in 1963 we had projectors in many of our trucks as we crisscrossed Europe reaching millions with the Word of God. We have been using video in a major way ever since. I soon discovered that almost all those films were criticized especially by people in the film world. Of course most were low budget and so there were great limitations. History and heaven will show how multitudes came to know Jesus through these films. Does this not show us how God's thinking is so different from ours? We long for great things and better films of course, but meanwhile God is using what we would reject to bring people to Himself. Are we not way more judgmental and narrow-minded than the living God?

Church Buildings: Some of the largest new church movements of our day also still have, to me, an unhealthy infatuation with extravagant buildings. The money that is poured into church buildings, while people are dying of hunger and living in poverty all around us, is something that many cannot understand. This has been a dividing line in the Christian world for hundreds of years—it is not new. Whole movements were born partly reacting to it like the Salvation Army and the Methodists. These movements and many others spread their faith around the world and so even in modern day India and Pakistan we have huge buildings often tied up in legal cases, generally run-down and looking very ugly.

Yes, be careful if you're going to say that God is not working among the people in some of the buildings today. It's a problem for me, but I don't really think it's a big deal with God. Some people get really upset if the old buildings are sold and become something else—especially a mosque. I personally think God is far more concerned about the people, including Muslims, than He is about the old building. Why are we not loving and reaching out to our Muslim neighbors with the gospel? Some of the churches that have been closed have been spiritually dead for years, turning away from the truth of Scripture decades ago, so why are we so worried? Even in places like the UK we have thousands of new churches and all kinds of Christian groups and surely that is more about what is on the heart of God today. There is a place for church buildings and I am sure all kinds of other buildings, but God will lead different people in different ways. I often find it upsetting but I don't think it's such a big deal with God.

Chapter 6

MUST WE BE
SO DOGMATIC?

I t is hard for us strong-minded, committed, Bible-believing Christians to ever change. But if we have been wrong, that is what we must do. Once we get set in our ways and in our theology, we almost never change. Without making some changes we can often become spiritually stuck and ineffective, often out of contact with the younger generation. Without change the vision and ministry won't be passed along to the next generation.

We are greatly influenced by the particular denomination, theological lens, or Bible college where we grew the most. We graduates might feel we have all our doctrine in cement. We sometimes think we have the answer to everything, even the hardest questions of life and theology. This to me is a great mistake. We must keep learning and growing, which often means admitting we are wrong. On the very basics of the Christian faith we must remain unmoveable, but on many issues in which there are a variety of interpretations, I believe it is better to not be so dogmatic. If we are to, as the Bible says, "Esteem others better than ourselves," then I think we must become more open to listening to others and be willing to change.

I have met so many people who are not interested that I am a believer in Jesus and saved by His grace. They seem to be more interested in whether I am Reformed, or charismatic, or Arminian, or Baptist, and the list goes on. Others want to know what I believe about the end times or the Jews or what translation of the Bible I use. I am not saying all this is irrelevant, but does it really please the Lord? Does this kind of mentality bring glory to God, which should always be what we want the most? Is there any hope for old guys like me who, after almost sixty years of studying biblical doctrine and theology, are still not sure exactly what the truth is on some controversial issues? Many of these issues are dividing lines between great leaders who I respect on both sides.

All my life I have struggled with the fact that so many who study theology lose their way and no longer believe the

Bible is the Word of God. Sometimes referred to as "liberal theology," it became dominant going way back to the 1920s and 30s in so many seminaries and colleges. Can we even begin to understand the impact of that in places like Germany, Switzerland, the Netherlands, and even Sri Lanka and India, and of course the United States? In light of this, should not those of us who believe the Bible stand in unity and not let so many smaller issues divide us? Embracing messiology will help us do that for sure.

If there is more humility and less hyper-dogmatism on minor and controversial issues, then there would be fewer people reacting to it and falling into the deep pond of unbelief. In the end, people who are too dogmatic sometimes lose their faith altogether. History proves this, and I could have been one of them.

So, what's the answer? Change of attitude? Yes. More humility? Yes. And a different view of what God wants from us and our minds. Surely more fruit of the Holy Spirit and fewer unkind dogmatic remarks. Will we ever face the clear truth that without love we are *nothing*? Can there be more listening and higher esteem for those who believe differently, especially if they are people who believe the Bible is the Word of God?

The Pentecostal and charismatic movements, which are some of the largest movements in the entire two-thousand-year history of the church, have long been polarizing. I have always written against extremes and so have many Pentecostals, such as Lee Grady of *Charisma* magazine. This part of the body of Christ seems vulnerable, to say the least. But in my view they are one of the most faithful movements (with an incredible variety of denominations and churches) to believe the Bible is God's Word and with it faithfully preaching the gospel. That is why tens of millions have come to Jesus through their efforts and in answer to prayer.

Yes, they often add other teachings, some of which I believe are wrong. But that is true of most churches and movements in history. Surely God in His mercy still saves people in the midst of it all, and I think saving people is what really is on the heart of God. In order to drive forward our other teachings, and Pentecostals are very good at it, we underestimate the importance of so great a salvation. I do find it a struggle that when my Pentecostal and charismatic friends are under attack they fall into the same pit of being too dogmatic about things that are not that clear in the Bible and on which great men and women of faith have not agreed for centuries.

One group often attacks another group by telling horror

stories about certain people in their tradition who have failed and sinned in major ways. But like I said before, you cannot prove that your view is right, or that someone else's is wrong, by cherry picking horror stories of people on the opposing side who have erred. At the same time, these stories of failure and sin must not be ignored. God commands us to think more on that which is "right and good and of good report" (Philippians 4:8). A leading conservative mission society has had workers convicted and imprisoned for pedophilia, which breaks our hearts, but that does not prove anything about the mission and the rest of the people. Just this morning I was studying about David, Saul, and Solomon. If you read Gordon MacDonald's brilliant book *Rebuilding Your Broken World*, you will see that most Old Testament saints had what he calls "broken world experiences." Yes, there are many areas where we need to be strong and unmovable (some like the word "dogmatic") but let's always stay humble, teachable and ready to change and become more like Christ.

Do we only care for people when it's part of our job or do we really care for people because of the revolutionary work of *grace* in our hearts? This leads me to another question. Do we mainly care for people when they are part of our organization, so that after they leave us in a few years we hardly remember their names, or do we make a commitment to love and care no matter where they may go? My surveys show that after leaving a ministry or organization, many people soon feel forgotten. Oh, how the devil knows how to exploit that! He tries to get them to believe the organization only used them. Most people say they don't have time to keep in touch with so many, but when I study people's lives and see how they waste time, it blows my mind. It's hard for us to face our own self-centeredness and lack of real dynamic, forgiving, and practical love. I write this also for myself as I am a pilgrim, failure, and learner!

Chapter 7

MY STORY: ROMANCE, MONEY, AND MUCH MERCY

I think by the age of thirteen, romance became the biggest thing in my life—right up there with sports and making money. The first girl I dated became my steady girlfriend. I think after dancing lessons we went to see *Quo Vadis*, and only eternity will tell what kind of influence that film had on my young life. Around that same time, dear Mrs. Clapp, who lived across from my high school, put my name on her "Holy Ghost Hit List," not only praying that I would become a Christian but also a missionary. Wow, she did not even discuss this with me! I actually had other plans for my life. I was already in business and that's where I was headed.

This amazing girl, Lynn, was a good influence on me. She went to a Baptist Church and I had no idea what that was. I remember her showing me the baptistry, which seemed really strange. I got to know and appreciate her parents, and they all were a good influence in my life. After we broke up there were so many different girls who blew my romantic circuits, and I moved, in a small way, into the world of pornography and lust. At the same time the gospel of John, sent by Mrs. Clapp and her son Danny, broke into my life, and in my semi-liberal Reformed Church I had a godly Sunday school teacher, Fred Gnade, who was to become a lifelong friend.

A Billy Graham Crusade on March 3, 1955, made all the difference. That night I was born from above and everything began to change. I was new to the family of God and soon discovered how much its values and lifestyle differ from the world's principles. It seemed I was no longer allowed to kiss or dance, but I did not find any verses on that, so I kept doing both.

I was now seventeen and had my own car, a Henry J (wow, that really dates me!). As a senior in high school I fell head over heels for a girl who was younger and went to an Episcopalian Church. God was pursuing me big time as I was in the Word and starting to evangelize the high school where I had been elected president of student council.

Around that same time, I did a really stupid thing. Parked off the road, and sort of in the woods, my girlfriend and I started kissing. As I began having ideas about what might come next, the police banged on the window, and in my panic I backed the car into a ditch. That was the worst night in my teenage years; her dad came to rescue us and, maybe due to his having had a few drinks, accused me of things we did not do. As you might guess, that relationship was soon over.

Then it happened again, only this time it was in a church parking lot and it brought an end to wild romance in my life. I am sure it's because people were praying. I decided on a "cold turkey fast," with no dating and no kissing. This went on for almost two years. Then I met Drena, who became my wife.

Though I originally chose to go to Maryville College, partly because they had dancing after lunch every day, I never danced or dated there. Rather, it was there that much of the early growth in my Christian life took place. I was on fire for Jesus. Every extra hour I had I was out in evangelism or praying, reading the Word, or going to a Christian meeting. In an amazing way a Baptist pastor in a country church let me preach. Then the door opened for ministry in the Blount County Jail, which opened the door when I was only 18 to share at the Nashville State Penitentiary. Great books came into my life like *Passion for Souls* by Oswald Smith and *Through Gates of Splendor* by Elisabeth Elliot and many more. I was greatly impacted doing a correspondence course on how to lead people to Christ. When that same Baptist pastor took me to my first mission conference down the road in Chattanooga, I was never the same again. As I found out about more nations and how so many were unreached, the vision for reaching them (especially the Muslims) began to grow in my heart and mind. When I started to realize that finance was urgently needed, I starting selling everything I could and gave the money to world missions. I got a job waiting on tables in the college restaurant in order to be able to give more.

It was during this period we first went to Mexico in the summer of 1957. I was soon speaking basic Spanish and the impact of what I saw caused me to want to leave the liberal arts at Maryville College and go to Moody Bible Institute in Chicago. I especially wanted to live and evangelize in the big city. I'd had a taste of it near my home when I went distributing thousands of tracts in the subway in New York City and then I got involved in the famous Billy Graham campaign in the summer of '57 just before we went to Mexico. I even preached in the streets there.

Arriving at a place like Moody was a big shock, especially

seeing so many attractive girls. I must have been infatuated with several in the first week, but I kept my romance fast. Looking back, I wonder if I had tried to kiss one if they would have hit me with their big King James Bible. Of course Moody had a strict rulebook, so I never had to find out.

One day passion for evangelism led me to get a film from the Moody Institute of Science office up on the 7th or 8th floor—and that walk up the stairs changed my life. Drena was sitting at the desk in charge of that office. When I saw her, my romantic circuits blew and I broke my fast, moving in on the target. For me it was love at first sight, but as soon as I said something rather stupid, for her it was fright at first sight. But she did agree to meet. That's when I told her, "Well, nothing probably is going to happen between me and you, but if anything did, like say marriage, you need to understand that I am going to be a missionary and you probably will be eaten by cannibals in New Guinea." How she eventually agreed to marry me is a long story, including a difficult summer together in Mexico City, then leaving her behind when we all went back to Moody. This led to my best Mexican friend falling in love with her and phoning me up to ask if that was okay. Wow, this led me to serious fasting and prayer. After a phone call with Drena, she was soon on a long bus journey back to Chicago. Phew!

In all this I was deeply convicted of my lack of practical love and sensitivity. Drena was discovering herself and her deep emotional needs. Our engagement might have broken if it were not for a deep experience she had with Jesus in the quiet of her own room, as she understood something of the all-sufficiency of Christ. This also led to a healing experience of some physical symptoms that had bothered her for a long time.

We will never forget that big day, January 31, 1960, when we got married. We did not have anything fancy (Keep in mind that Drena's stepfather Henry was not a Christian. The story of his conversion to Jesus many years later is something we will always thank God for). We had the marriage ceremony right after the Sunday morning service of Lake Drive Baptist Church. They did not have their own building, so this was in a school gymnasium. Walter Borchard was my best man. A bus came up from Chicago with our friends, mainly Moody students. Dale preached a powerful message at the reception mentioning that the main thing they could do for us was pray as we probably would sell all the gifts for world missions. How I wish we had not lost the old reel-to-reel tape with that message.

Back around 1970 I was going to write a book about marriage and had the title *The Revolutionary Marriage* and even had an outline. But the truth is that then I needed to learn more about making our own marriage work before writing about it. So now that that time has come in part, here are some of the lessons I learned along the way:

Base it on the Bible. This has been the practical foundation of our marriage, always wanting Christ at the center of everything. Living on the floor in the back of our Mexico City bookstore was bringing some challenges and I was to learn fast that marriage was really God's PhD program in sanctification. We read "Revival in the Home," one of the chapters in *Calvary Road* by Roy Hession and learned more about brokenness, humility, and the Spirit-filled, crucified life. Over all these years, again and again I knew I had just the right person to be my life partner, and by His grace we have been totally faithful to one another. From the Bible we saw no other alternative.

Think differently about love. We write, preach about, and try to practice 1 Corinthians 13 along with other scriptures as the foundation for our marriage. I especially tend toward insensitivity and God has had to break and deal with me. Impatience has also been a problem throughout my life. Thankfully, the miracle of grace that set me free from anger in the earliest days of my walk with God has been a major factor in our walk together and in my leadership of the movement. There were still occasional failures that had to be quickly repented of, and to this day I feel sad about the times I hurt my wife and later my children with a burst of anger or an unkind word. Arriving in England from Spain, where our first son Benjamin was born, was a big step for us. At that time I read *Seven Deadly Sins* by Billy Graham, and how I thank the Lord for that book. I used to read his radio sermons all the time as a young Christian. Other books by him, like *Peace with God* and *The Secret of Happiness*, were all keys in laying a spiritual foundation in my life.

God owns everything. Our desire to reach people with God's Word both locally and around the world, combined with starting a whole new missionary movement, always brought financial pressure. These challenges gave me a zeal that God seemed to use, but that also seemed to confuse some people—including my own wife. I emphasized Luke 14:33: *In the same way, those of you who do not give up everything you have cannot be my disciples.* That challenge had already led us to sell most of our possessions. Others followed us in this but it sometimes led to being judgmental of those who seemed to be wasting money. We needed the balance that Philippians 4:19 would supply. We were starting to learn more about the mystery of how things that seem so good can have a dark side. Gray started to come into our more black-and-white world and has been on the increase ever since. Can you guess why the last verses of Romans 11 have been so important to us?

> *Oh, the depth of the riches of the wisdom and*
> *knowledge of God!*
> *How unsearchable his judgments,*
> *and his paths beyond tracing out!*
> *Who has known the mind of the Lord?*
> *Or who has been his counselor?"*
> *Who has ever given to God,*
> *that God should repay them?"*
> *For from him and through him and for him are*
> *all things.*
> *To him be the glory forever! Amen.*

Prayers sometimes go unanswered (and sometimes they get answered). The biggest mystery as we moved down the marriage road was seeing so much unanswered prayer, even in areas that are hard to talk about. We started to battle large attacks of discouragement and disappointment. The years with three children living in India, the years in Kathmandu, Nepal, and then on the OM ship *Logos* gave us endless opportunities to learn and grow together. I felt

Drena's help and affirmation through it all and remember very few complaints even in the heat of the battle. Depression somehow came into Drena's life in the mid-70s, which took us all by surprise. A woman confronted me during that time pointing out that I was probably part of the problem. God broke me and showed me changes that needed to take place in my own life, including the way I behaved as a husband and father. After a year, Drena came out of this dark period and it never came back. We are sad at the simplistic answers some Christians gave to these complex illnesses and, in my view, misguided teaching on healing (although I do believe God heals) has hurt more people and the body of Christ as a whole more than we will ever know.

Criticism will come. Handling criticism is an important part of leadership and I sometimes found it difficult and felt personally hurt. I never heard much criticism of our marriage or my wife, but we found it hard to handle what we did hear, often second-hand. A major part of leadership and your walk with God will be tested to the core when your marriage is criticized. In God's mercy, I am sure some of the worst gossip and criticism we never do hear, especially if you're in the fast lane trying to evangelize the whole world. I was greatly blessed by always having people like Dale Rhoton and Peter Maiden and others, who I know often came to my defense. It is much harder for leaders who do not have such faithful friends and coworkers. As I look back I realize I learned so much from my critics and from close friends who would walk in the light with me about something they saw in my life and ministry that needed change. God showed us from His Word and other books that it is not possible to do anything without criticism. We always tried to love our critics and ask God's blessing on them. We were never surprised at the power of gossip. The truth is that we were/are happy and fulfilled most of the time, and right into these unique senior years when many things change—especially in the area of health. We are blessed to have so many people praying for us, and some of you who are reading this are in that category. We thank you with all our hearts and hope you will keep on praying.

Balance is key. Balance became one of the most important words in our lives. Balance between work and family. Balance between taking in and giving out. Balance between giving and receiving. Balance in terms of going the extra mile to reach more people and slowing down to have family fun together. In my old Bible I had a couple of lists that were working for balance.

Children and grandchildren always help bring about change in your life. We are thankful to God for our three children, five grandchildren, and two great-grandchildren. We love them and try to be the best parents (and now grandparents) we can be. We have wonderful and amazing times together, including trips, holidays, and vacations.

And we are very aware of failure and realize the subtlety of what I now call *unrealistic destructive idealism*. When we set unrealistically high goals as we have, we will fail. Some non-Christians would not even think of some of these things as failures. This is why books like Philip Yancey's *What's So Amazing About Grace?* have been so important to us. And what about the breath of fresh air from the *Ragamuffin Gospel* by Brennan Manning? In those early days especially, legalism had entered our movement and also our home and damage was done. We now have to practice 1 Peter 5:7 and cast it upon Him, accepting His forgiveness. Without radical forgiveness, radical discipleship will never work.

Chapter 8

NOT JUST SIN, BUT MISTAKES COST

I owe so much to my parents who may not have known Jesus personally during my childhood, but who had many Christian values and taught us right from wrong. They helped me learn how to work hard, which laid a vital foundation in my life before I ever came to Jesus. Working hard at school, in sports, and in Boy Scouts also helped me more than I realize. The Scouts sent me on an advanced leadership training course when I was very young. Tell me, do you think the living God was preparing me for something I could have never imagined?

I learned quickly that mistakes are costly and they often

bring difficulty in more ways than one. As a little boy, I made the mistake of balancing a penny on my nose, which I proceeded to swallow. My mother insisted that I come home from school every time I had to go to the toilet. The Washington Primary School was near our home in Wyckoff, New Jersey, and so we got the penny back! I made another mistake on a frozen lake during ice skating season and fell through the ice. Thank God someone was there to pull me out.

All my life, especially after becoming a follower of Jesus, I have been an avid reader. While I have read books, newspapers, magazines, articles, and now endless email attachments, no reading material has been more important than God's Word, the Bible. The Bible is filled with stories of great success and great failures and we can learn from both.

It seems that no matter where you read in the Bible you are always reading about mistakes people make (unless you are reading about Jesus!). I think as believers in Jesus it is important that we don't think all mistakes are sin. They may have some roots in our fallen nature, but they are not always outright sin needing repentance. Satan likes to use our mistakes to get us discouraged or down on ourselves. When we allow ourselves to get discouraged we open ourselves up to sin or wrong attitudes and behavior—that is when we get into much more trouble spiritually. When we make a mistake, we must bounce back, look for plan B, and press on. We could all be helped by the book *Second Choice* by Viv Thomas.

History shows the domino effect of mistakes, with one mistake leading to another. We lost our first ship *Logos* (which was once home for our whole family!) on some submerged rocks in the Beagle Channel in the very south of Chile and Argentina. Our analysis showed a series of mistakes by different people which led to that fateful day in 1988. God was merciful and there was no loss of life—and He even used the publicity from that event to help get the funds and people for a much better ship, *Logos II*, which later led to *Logos HOPE*.

History also shows that everyone makes mistakes. Of course, the fewer mistakes the better. We must not allow what we believe about the sovereignty of God, or about what I call *messiology*, to keep us from a strong common sense commitment to do things right and make as few mistakes as possible. I wish that I had been warned at Bible college just how hard life is and how many problems and difficulties we would all face. We need to reread and study passages like James 1 and 1 Peter 1. I never realized how just having the money to buy food is such a huge issue for so many people. I sometimes gave the false impression that if you prayed enough or had enough faith, everything would work out okay.

Now looking back at sixty years in Christ, for so many people I have worked with over the years it has *not turned out okay*! Many have not been successful in their ministry or jobs or even in their marriages. There are quite a few who after the faith, prayer, and evangelistic life of OM, returned home and could not get a job or hold one down. Some of the marriages of people who met in OM have broken, often because they had not thought about the problems they would face in the future. Put this together with other mistakes we easily make and you have a formula for trouble—often big trouble. I meet such people all the time and try to share radical grace. I say, "If you have failed and missed plan A, then praise the Lord that plan B can be just as good." Some have made many mistakes and had many failures and feel they are probably on plan H or M. I say, "Praise the Lord for a big alphabet." People usually laugh at this point but in the end, the truth is that some of those mistakes could have been avoided. While embracing radical grace, we must also beware of fatalism in any of its forms. Some of our mistakes are rooted in sin, while others reveal a lack of wisdom and discernment. One of the reasons I have read so widely is to learn from the mistakes and failures of others, and in my lifetime I have read about thousands of them.

How can we avoid mistakes?

Saturate ourselves with God's Word, giving ourselves to prayer in all aspects of our spiritual walk with God. I have emphasized this in all my books.

Learn discipline in all the basic areas of life—while also steering clear of legalism every step of the way.

Read and study hard. Have a system to remember important information.

Write things down. If you travel, have a list of things you must not forget. Our phones and other gadgets can help, but it still demands discipline.

Plan ahead and count the cost, as we are urged to do in the last verses of Luke 14. I could write a whole chapter on this important concept as some of the biggest mistakes I have seen are in this area. Many people have come to me and shared about their great vision and dreams but most of them never materialize or last long. Often they did not count the cost or were not ready to pay the price. When you have time, try to think of the pros and cons for a particular step or action you are about to take.

Seek advice. It's especially helpful to talk with several trusted mentors, which can help you avoid (or at least spot) wrong advice.

Learn how to check on one another and learn from each other. Walk in humility and let pride die, ready to quickly confess weakness.

Develop good systems. Have a good system with back-up for all addresses, phone numbers, etc. Have a system for filing things. The folders on my laptop are now a key part of my life. What a great tool to use in God's work. I have a little black back-up book for phone numbers—I use it all the time! If we really love people and want to encourage them, we will go the extra mile to keep their basic information. Gordon MacDonald's book *Ordering Your Private World* has helped a lot of people. If you read widely you will find practical advice on almost every aspect of life and it is a great mistake not to learn from it.

Learn what I call "Holy Ghost Caution." There was a wonderful missionary who was out walking in the hills of England, but he did not have on the right kind of shoes. He walked too close to the edge of a cliff, slipped, and fell to his death. I will never forget getting the phone call the next day about this dear friend's death. The problem is, I could share another few hundred similar stories that I know about. That is why I am taking time to write this book and especially this chapter.

You may think such ordinary concerns are not as important as insights about the Christian life and discipleship, but separating the so-called sacred from the practical is a great mistake in our thinking. You decide each hour of every day what you will do, where you will go, and how you will behave. We must bring it all together under the power and guidance of the Holy Spirit. Even at my age there are lessons to learn.

Each great biblical reality and teaching must be re-learned at different phases of our lives. We must not just live well, but learn and be ready to die well. As we get older we must remember these great words from James 1:22: *Do not merely listen to the word, and so deceive yourselves. Do what it says.*

Chapter 9

THE LEADERS
GOD USES

I am typing this chapter in a special place on the west coast
of Wales, called the Hookses. This is where one of the great
Christian leaders of the twentieth century—Dr. John Stott—
did a lot of his writing. He became a close friend, and his
books to this day have global influence. It's sad that, especially in the US, if you mention John's name some people will
bring up how he denied the existence of hell (particularly
eternal punishment), which is not true at all. He believed
people outside of Christ were lost. I spoke to him personally
about it. In one of his books, written especially to answer the
tough questions that some liberal theologians were asking,
he touched on the possibility of some kind of annihilation

and we also spoke with each other about this. Many great men and women of God have struggled with exactly what hell is like. I remember Billy Graham saying it was mainly separation from God.

I have tried to live my entire life since my conversion in the light of this truth, which I still don't fully understand. I have been helped by meditating on the justice of God. Universalism is more popular than ever, but John Stott did not go down that road, and I am sure it's one of the reasons he was so committed to global missions. I heard him say in a missions message that one of the great battles of the church in our day was the exclusiveness of the gospel. Jesus is the Way, the Truth and the Life and no man comes to the Father but by Him (John 14:6).

That leads me to the main thrust of this chapter. Consider the wide range of people God uses in leadership, both men and women. Can you imagine the number of leaders I have met and in whose churches I have spoken? Add to this all the different kinds of leaders I have known in missions agencies and other organizations. Yes, it's in the thousands, and yes I have listened to thousands of messages. This doesn't even count the leadership messages from the Bible!

We have a huge range of books on leadership and endless autobiographies and biographies of men and women of God right back to the beginning of time. They are now coming at us faster than ever and one of the most important parts of my own ministry is speaking to leaders and also distributing outstanding leadership materials. My two top books at present are *Spiritual Leadership* by J. Oswald Sanders and *Leading with Love* by Alex Strauch.

I have expressed some of my views strongly in *Grace Awakened Leadership*, which in fact is two key chapters taken from my book *Out of the Comfort Zone.*

Again, if you don't embrace what I call *messiology* you will probably not agree with what I am trying to share here. I am strongly convinced that God works mightily through a wide range of different leaders and different leadership styles.

Some books and teachers have very high ideals for leadership and some are so dogmatic that styles different from their own are condemned or looked down upon. I try to warn people about what I call destructive idealism, which leaves out the radical grace factor and eventually leaves people discouraged, confused, or even wiped out completely.

History proves otherwise. All kinds of leaders and leadership teams have been mightily used to bless, disciple, and teach His people as well as bring tens of millions to the Lord Jesus around the globe. We are key distributors of Chua Wee Hian's book *Servant Leadership*, but also for decades watched how he led a key church that he founded in London after being the international leader of the whole of the International Fellowship of Evangelical Students movement. Put that with David Lundy's book *Servant Leadership for Slow Learners* and you have a unique combination. I have noticed that many leaders who have actually accomplished the most have not followed that style. They often have been more autocratic and some get accused of being dictatorial or even abusive. I read a book about abusive leadership in which, as far as I could see, almost every dynamic leader who tries to persuade people with some passion and emotion to serve and love Jesus with heart, mind, soul, and strength, will be considered abusive. Some people, when they come under that kind of person, do not want to accept the strong message and will try to find weakness in the person giving the message. If we are honest, there are some verses that seem to be a tad harsh like: *I know your deeds, that you are neither cold nor hot. I wish you were either one or the other! So, because you are lukewarm—neither hot nor cold—I am about to spit you out of my mouth* (Revelation 3:15–16). And then Luke 14:33: *In the same way, those of you who do not give up everything you have cannot be my disciples.*

We really need a lot of wisdom on how we use that strong word "abusive." I remember someone on one of our teams years ago who I thought was rushing into marriage. When I suggested caution, this person turned on me and accused me of being a control freak. After that hurtful conversation, I stood with them and even attended their wedding and reception only to see the marriage come to an end a few years later.

One thing for sure that I must say after sixty years in leadership is that, at its best, it is very difficult. All of us as leaders are imperfect and have our weaknesses that sometimes lead to clear-cut sin. All the people we try to lead and help also have weaknesses leading sometimes to sin, so the result will often be one big mess! Hurt people, broken hearts, and disappointments. So many who come under our leadership today have already been hurt so much, sometimes even sexually abused, that it's extremely hard to lead and help them. Most leaders are busy and overcommitted, and often it's because they are trying to love and serve Jesus and His people. Add to that an effort to evangelize and have many non-Christian friends and you are looking at the impossible. Things will go wrong. People will be hurt. That is why, without the burning reality of 1 Corinthians 13 flowing in our hearts and the humility and brokenness that go with it, it often becomes impossible to move forward. I have seen and read of hundreds of leaders who have fallen out with each other. I have seen a number two leader try to a pull a coup and overthrow the so-called number one.

It takes a high level of spiritual maturity for leaders to work together.

Is God still at work even in the midst of our broken churches filled with broken people? Two thousand years of church history show that God is doing great things and saving multitudes of people in the midst of sinful, messy situations.

Let's beware of being too narrow in terms of the way we feel God works through people. We can have our convictions on how we should lead, but be slow to criticize people who have a different style. Different churches have all kinds of leadership styles. Yes, I personally believe some are better than others, but these things are much harder to measure than I once assumed. There is hardly a single church or Christian mission or organization that has not had its messes and its problems and yes, its sinful behavior. In some cases I make a firm decision to pull back and stay away. *But I cannot tell the living God to stay away.* He will continue to amaze us with the way He uses all kinds of leaders in all kinds of situations, including the very messy ones. Yes, it's *messiology* on a grand scale.

Chapter 10

WORSHIP, WALKING, AND BALANCE

I have just been walking and worshiping here by the Hookses where John Stott must have often walked, prayed, and watched the birds. I took a look in his office and saw that many of his books were on the shelves, including his two-volume biography. I even found a new book I had not seen before called *John Stott: A Portrait by His Friends*. It's edited by Chris Wright who is now the leader of the Langham Partnership. Wish I could just sit down and read it all.

I have walked this area many times. Walking and, for quite a few years, jogging have been important parts of my life. I often combine them with praise, prayer, and worship. I find it easier to worship out in the midst of God's creation than in a building filled with people, but of course I believe in both. Being alone with God has been a major part of my handling stress and all the challenges of leadership. I am especially fascinated by water, canyons, gorges, and rugged coast lines.

My favorite places (competing with the Swiss Alps while on the trains dictating letters) are all the national and state parks in southern Utah and northern Arizona, including Bryce, the Arches, Zion, and the Grand Canyon. God in His mercy and love has let me visit these places many times with various people including my children and grandchildren.

I am actually sitting on an inside window ledge looking out over the beautiful coastline with Milford Haven somewhere in the distance, where I remember the *Logos* visiting many decades ago. It is my prayer that many of you will read *The Logos Story*, *The Doulos Story*, and now *Logos HOPE*. You will be amazed at how the Lord has used these ships to do His work. My mind jumps back to when John Stott and I ministered together on *Logos II* in London. He and I were very different, and when he first heard me speak at Urbana in the late 60s he was quite upset with the lack of Bible content in my message (it was mainly my testimony). When he confronted me I started crying. Little did we know that it was the beginning of a lifelong friendship. The more we spoke or ministered together the more we realized how much we had in common and he became a great supporter of OM. What a joy to have preached recently to All Souls Church where he was the leader and rector for so many years.

I write all of this to encourage people to find balance in their lives. I hope you have read about this in some of my other books, but I cannot overemphasize the importance of it, especially finding the right balance between the aspects of work and ministry that you find quite draining and those aspects that refuel you.

Even in your Bible study it is vital to let one strong Scripture be brought to its true perspective by other Scriptures. Taking verses out of context, especially from the Old Testament, and hitting people on the head with them is not the way to go. I never cease to be amazed at the misuse of Scripture. We of course take the passages we like and leave out those we don't like or understand. People can get caught up with misguided views often circulated by one-sided emails or websites that take verses out of context and seldom give the full picture.

When I meet such people, they are sometimes very negative, or even bitter and angry. Talking to these people makes me think that selective reading (reading only one side of issues) is worse than not reading at all. Everyone with any

education and experience knows you cannot believe everything you read; even Christian books, magazines, and papers
exaggerate or get it wrong sometimes. Even some major
papers are dominated by only one viewpoint. There are endless cults and extremist groups propagating their "thing" all
over the world. Apologies sometimes come, but so often in
such small print that most people miss them. Some popular emails and blogs have been proven totally false. All kinds
of conspiracy theories are flying around, some as old as the
hills. Health, religion, and politics are the big areas of endless generalizations, half-truths, overreactions, and pure
nonsense.

When people are locked into a particular political party
(not necessarily wrong) they find it impossible to see any
positives that the other parties may be saying or doing. I
often find such a lack of balance in what people say, and that
includes a lot of the preaching that I have listened to. People
are often unable to understand how much their own tem-
perament and experiences affect what they believe and speak
about. Of course, black-and-white thinkers are especially
vulnerable in this world of so much gray. As committed believers in Jesus and His Word, we know certain things are
clearly black-and-white. Thou shalt not kill, for example. Yet
even there Christians are not always in agreement, especially

about weapons and war. I have upset some people when, after they set forth their great opinion about something, I point out the complexity.

Can we not—even with our strong convictions—be humble and realize we might be wrong? Can we not read more sides to an issue? (I realize this is hard work in our fast-lane, "send-a-text" world.)

Should we not learn from scholars and especially godly men and women as they write and share on almost every subject in the world? The generalizations about Muslims (and many other peoples) that often include prejudice and hateful language should be a concern to all of us. Some books are feeding the fire and many people now claim to know a lot about Islam. I may be wrong, but I see so much pride, impatience, and arrogance and so little of Jesus, humility, and brokenness.

It sometimes is a huge stumbling block for those who are trying to reach these different peoples with the gospel. When we meet someone we don't agree with, say on a political or doctrinal issue, are we more concerned about changing their viewpoint than we are seeing them come to Jesus? Or if they are a believer, extending our love, fellowship, and listening to their story? One reason some people have few friends is that they do not really love people or listen to them. They just press on in their own views, looking down on those who are not in agreement. The missing word with too many today is "repent", which involves a U-turn and life change.

In the midst of the mess we see all around, even in the church and Christian organizations, how do we press on and stay encouraged and positive? Of course there are whole books and sermons that answer this, but for me it must include messiology. It was hard for me as a Christian leader to admit that I had a wrong view of God and the way He works among His people. What about you?

Chapter 11

IF YOU DON'T WANT TO GET HURT, DON'T PLAY RUGBY

I was having lunch with Paul Dando, a pastor in Wales, who leads a church in Narberth where I have spoken many times. I remember being there one time with my grandson Charlie who helped me at my book table. Charlie had never done this before and was surprised that he could not keep all the money people gave us.

Paul shared the following story in a little restaurant in Little Haven. It was at a leaders meeting, and some of the leaders were really hurting from difficulties and people in their churches. Just before an older visiting speaker from

South Africa was about to bring the main message, one of them led in prayer and especially prayed for those who were hurting. The opening line of this seasoned leader's message was, "If you don't want to get hurt, don't play rugby." Oh, how true. Americans might want to say if you don't want to get hurt, don't play football.

All over the world I have told people and especially leaders if you don't want to get hurt you're on the wrong planet. This is the way our fallen and rebellious planet is, and we must learn how to press on in the midst of it. Even in the very best of healthy churches, mistakes will be made. People will sin and fail and people will need help. It does not make it any easier when we think of Satan as a roaring lion seeking someone to devour (1 Peter 5:8).

I have been helped and inspired by so many men and women who, through every kind of hurt and difficulty, have exercised forgiveness and pressed on. At the same time if we who are in leadership will live out the reality of the indwelling Holy Spirit, I believe we will personally hurt fewer people. I have often tried to find out if something I have said or done has hurt someone and then have gone out of the way to apologize and ask forgiveness. We need to ask ourselves how often we say, "I'm sorry; please forgive me." Should it not be basic to our heart and vocabulary?

Misunderstandings are basic to life on this planet. I have seen thousands of them both big and small. Destructive gossip is often released not because of some clear-cut sin or evil, but due to miscommunication or misunderstanding. All of our married life, Drena and I have struggled in this area. Most of the time it is a very small issue but the enemy tries to use it to bring confusion, hurt, and pain. We must learn how to counter this with better listening and a greater effort to understand the person talking or the one being talked about. The challenge to believe the best about someone is very important.

I want to bring in here my plea to make prayer and prayer meetings a central part of your life and ministry. One of the most important things I learned as a young Christian was how to pray and also to make prayer meetings a top priority, which I have maintained by His grace all my life. There are hundreds of books on prayer and I don't want to repeat what others have said, but I must remind you how prayerlessness will open the door for so many setbacks, problems, and hurts.

This leads me to share about one of the most important aspects of our walk with God and it's the challenge not to hold hurts or anything else against someone. By His grace I have never gone to bed with anything against people and

I have been hurt and disappointed by people hundreds of times. To me it's not an option. We must forgive and even work on forgetting. The verses about loving our enemies make it even more wrong and ridiculous to hold anything against someone. To seek to get even or take revenge has no place in the life of a disciple of our loving Lord. This does not mean there will be great fellowship or working together. That's often a more complex step that is not always possible. As we are more mature in our faith, and it was hard for me, we learn how to press on with unsolved relationship complexities. *How can two walk together unless they are in agreement?* That is a different level from basic love, respect, and forgiveness. We have to remind ourselves often that there is only one body. Yes, we are the body of Christ.

How can we possibly think we are going to evangelize the world and plant churches among all people without every kind of problem and trial that the mind can imagine, including some even losing their lives for the cause of Christ? The martyrs we have had in our movement have made a huge impact on most of us and helped us get our priorities sorted out for His glory. I would urge people to read Gary Witherall's book *Total Abandon* written after the martyrdom of his wife in Lebanon. With it please try reading R. T. Kendall's book *Total Forgiveness*. Serving in God's great global army is going to be tougher than rugby or football. Remember 2 Timothy 2:3 (NKJV): *You therefore must endure hardship as a good soldier of Jesus Christ.* And while you're at it, read the whole chapter!

Chapter 12

MOANERS, COMPLAINERS, AND NEGATIVE THINKERS

D oes this chapter title speak about you? I hope not—it's really a deadly road and too many are walking on it. I think I had some of this as a young Christian and even later on as a husband, father, and Christian leader. In many ways, I'm very optimistic, though with a strong negative streak. It gets more complex as God seems to use some of my negative statements, especially about the state of the church and even the average Christian.

We had to learn the hard way that *radical discipleship without radical grace is often a hurtful, confusing dead-end street*, yet God did great things in the midst of our zeal, weakness, and failure.

I remember being in Pakistan shortly after the work was started there about forty years ago. A door opened for an important meeting in a cathedral in a major city. Key church leaders were coming, including the bishop of the Church of Pakistan. I was the main speaker and I remember an OM leader asking me to be careful what I said when I preached. I guess he knew I often said some offensive or even stupid things when preaching. I told him I would try my best. Then someone else asked if I could dress properly. Suits and ties were a big thing then (and even today) in the Church of Pakistan. I was never known for being well dressed but, wow, the next day I was there in suit and tie. I think I looked like an undertaker. This happened to be a time in my life when I was determined to be less negative even in dark or difficult situations. God kept it interesting, for as I was speaking a pigeon flew over me and dropped its load on my suit sleeve. What an embarrassment in front of the bishop and all those people, many hearing me for the first time. But God was doing a new thing and I just said, "Praise the Lord that elephants here don't fly." Of course there was great laughter.

Yes, you might be in a bad situation but why not thank and praise the Lord—it could be a lot worse. That does not mean you should verbally praise the Lord when someone is pouring out a hurtful, difficult situation to you. At that moment you need to remember Romans 12:15: *Rejoice with those who rejoice and weep with those who weep.* At the same time we might be rejoicing in our hearts knowing God can bring something beautiful out of a terrible situation. I am reading Hanna Miley's book about her life as a child coming to England on the famous trains that brought children from Germany before the Holocaust. The book is called *A Garland for Ashes* and it is the story of reconciliation with those who took the lives of her parents and so many more in the concentration camps of Germany during that horrific war. There are many other similar books that God can use to change our lives.

Why are so many strong Bible-believing people (and I am one of them) so quick to criticize—often before they even have the facts? Why are so many Christians moaning about so many things especially about their governments? What do we do with Philippians 4:4–7?

God does not want us to be moaning, complaining, negative, unthankful people. Please pause for a moment and allow the Holy Spirit to do a new work in your heart and life. I want to highlight how this is closely tied to negativity and anger. It was hard as a young believer to realize I had a hostility streak. I saw it come out in my speaking once and I immediately repented. It especially would come out in my driving (I found it better when I went by train)!

Wherever you live today you find people around you moaning and complaining all the time. What does it actually accomplish? To me it's very different from constructive criticism. I read a book called *Tough-Minded Optimist* as well as other similar books, which helped change my way of thinking.

Do you spend much time with these kinds of people? Be careful; it's contagious! People who always see the dark side are frequently very proud, know-it-all types, and yet that pride is often tied to insecurity, which makes it an even more dangerous combination. The other day I typed out a list of things I have heard Christians moan or complain about recently:

Oh, the music is too loud.
Oh, they are using the wrong translation of the Bible.
Oh, how can they dress like that in church?
Oh, the pastor preached too long.
Oh, I wonder why his wife dresses so fancy and what
    she is doing with her time?
Oh, this person is so fat and that person just talks
    too much.

Oh, he keeps forgetting to use deodorant.

Oh, did you notice the new expensive car the pastor just got?

Oh, I saw one of the elders in a pub the other day.

Oh dear, they had red wine in the communion glass.

Oh, I saw the pastor's son having a beer.

In my early days I remember Christians getting upset over women wearing lipstick or men having long hair. The list could go on. When we think and behave this way, what does it accomplish of eternal value? Do we not understand the importance of our disposition and attitude? I am reading a book on grace called *Pharisectomy: How to Joyfully Remove Your Inner Pharisee and Other Religiously Transmitted Diseases* by Peter Haas and you can imagine what that's about. We need to remember that God is not just concerned about what we do and say, but what we think. Attitude is a major part of our walk with Jesus.

In almost every situation and in almost every person there are positive and good things, and we should focus on that much more. It is also crucial to remember that *in the same way you judge others, you will be judged, and with the measure you use, it will be measured to you* (Matthew 7:2). What about that great rule: *So in everything, do to others what you would have them do to you, for this sums up the Law and the Prophets* (Matthew 7:12). This is such a huge emphasis in the Bible. How can we miss it?

Read 1 Thessalonians 5:16, *Rejoice always.* Or Philippians 4:8, *Finally, brothers and sisters, whatever is true, whatever is noble, whatever is right, whatever is pure, whatever is lovely, whatever is admirable—if anything is excellent or praiseworthy—think about such things.*

I learned a new word recently from a friend in the education world. A blocker is someone who thinks everything is fine, especially with their own work, and they block any effort for change. If we are to grow and be the people God wants us to be then we must keep learning and keep changing.

Complaining and criticizing one's wife or husband is so often the road to a broken relationship. I, by God's grace, have seldom criticized my wife in public and not that much in private, but have had to repent of indirect statements and sometimes humor that may have sown a wrong idea about her to those who heard or read it. I remember once in a message paying a great tribute to my wife in more than a few sentences and got criticized for that as well! Have you found that sometimes life is full of no-win situations? Wow, my negative streak just popped out again. Oh, may the Lord have mercy on us all.

Chapter 13

PROCLAMATION + SOCIAL CONCERN AND ACTION

C an the biggest change in one's life and theology come after that person is sixty years of age? Yes, and it happened to me and it happened to the movement that I helped start, Operation Mobilization.

We need to go back to John Stott, Billy Graham, and the 1974 World Congress on Evangelism in Lausanne, Switzerland, where thousands of Christian leaders from across the world met. I had a small seminar on the subject of Literature Evangelism and I think I missed some of the key messages. There was a great debate going on about how these two fit together and in the end the famous Lausanne Document declared they must come together: social action and proclamation. Many articles and books came out for and against the decision, but this Congress, plus many other people's books and movements changed the course of history. Keep in mind that some churches and missionaries were already way out front in combining these two aspects of ministry. Just look at General Booth and the Salvation Army!

Years before this, Operation Mercy had begun under Bertil Engqvist, a major leader in OM from Sweden. I remember giving the go-ahead on this especially with the hope that most of the funding would come out of Sweden.

Afghanistan was one of the key nations in our vision from the very beginning. This kind of ministry was the only way to function in that nation and also among the refugees over the border in Pakistan where Gordon Magney (founder of our work there and now buried in Kabul) carried on the work with his wife, Grace. They had an amazing ministry of caring for all kinds of physical needs and trying to bring the gospel at the same time. Not an easy task.

Joseph D'souza, who was the leader of the work in India, was one of the pacesetters of the whole movement to bring about this huge change. The Good Shepherd slum work with clinics and schools was historic in our movement, and now there are over 110 much larger schools across the nation especially for the Dalit children who are so often denied a proper education. Over 200 million in India are considered untouchable. Many believe it is a form of slavery. We are not speaking of low caste people (of which there are hundreds of millions more), but those of an even lower social status—outcasts. Our concern for these people helped change the course of our history. This situation should not exist in what is called the world's largest democracy, but it does, and in God's mysterious way of working in one of the world's messiest situations, hundreds of thousands of these people are coming to Jesus.

During my exercise walks I have been listening to Philip Yancey's book *What's So Amazing About Grace?,* especially the part about segregation. We now wonder how that generation, including some professing Christians, could have been so blind, racist, and hateful. It seems unreal.

The new generation in South Africa is amazed at what their parents believed and practiced (praise Jesus for every exception) in those days known as apartheid. When they watch films or read the history they find it hard to believe and often feel ashamed.

Here is my big question to all who read this: what issues today do we have so wrong that future generations will stand in amazement at our blindness, prejudice, laziness, or stupidity?

Wow, now there's a finger pointing at me!

I believe one of these issues is *untouchability*. This system has created a group of people who are living in a form of slavery and apartheid with hyper-segregation. As this goes on, it affects the daily lives of over 200 million people, mainly in India, but other nations as well.

Where do you stand on this issue? What are you and I doing about it? We should ask ourselves the question: what will our children and grandchildren be saying about us in the future?

I lived in India and missed it, but I thank God for those who helped me wake up so that one of the major goals in my life is to see this changed.

The next step for some of you may be to read Joseph D'souza's book *Dalit Freedom Now and Forever*.

In 1998, at our annual leaders conference in South Africa, I announced that in five years I would step out of the international leadership of the movement. That took place in the summer of 2003.

As I transitioned out of leadership some were thinking, "That Verwer, Mr. Proclamation-Evangelization, he'll never change!" Imagine their surprise as God moved me to embrace this theology of ministry. I saw it clearly in the Bible and in history. This has changed the way I think and speak and live. It especially changed how I use my time and money. In our Special Project Ministry, which Peter Maiden and the leaders of OM felt I should keep and lead as part of OM, we began to get involved in more projects connected with global social concerns from the AIDS crisis to the impure water problem and every possible struggle connected with poverty. I realized as I moved down the road of more concern for human rights that this must include the rights of the unborn. Linked with Patrick Dixon we flooded out a couple hundred thousand copies of his book *AIDS Action* in many languages. With Randy Alcorn we moved tens of thousands of copies of *Why Pro-Life?* In some languages it was the first Christian book on that subject ever put into print. God opened doors to share this message all over the world, even on television, radio, and the Internet.

There is not space in this book to go into the details of the challenges and changes that faced us all in the movement as this took place. It has not been an easy marriage, but of course marriage never is. Some felt that basic evangelism was being pushed aside and that social action and relief projects were totally dominating the movement.

Debates took place and papers were written. The whole work seemed to become more complex and messy. The pressure to raise funds for crucial needs and crises seemed to be off the charts. Looking back, the provision of funds for so much great ministry in answer to prayer constantly amazes me. I am not sure that anyone knows how much bigger the annual budget is now in comparison to what some call the "old days." It's doubled a number of times. I sense we still have a good balance with evangelism and church planting still being at the very heart of what we do. The books and audiovisuals that come out of OM are clear. For example, in the case of my own ministry and special projects I speak about all these things, but since mine is a relatively small amount of money compared to OM's total income, I feel that most of it should be used for reaching millions with the gospel.

I am especially encouraged with the ship ministry and the way it keeps reaching people with the gospel—especially using literature. Over 40 million people have actually been up the gangway, and tens of millions more have been reached in onshore outreach and church ministry.

What moved me in the direction of social concern? First of all it was a deeper study of Scripture—both the Old and New Testament. Men of God like John Stott and others of a similar mind were a huge influence. Even some with whom I did not agree caused me to search my heart and be ready for radical change.

Yes, OM has become more complicated and some don't

like it and have abandoned us, but others are being raised up, especially of the younger generation to carry the work forward. One of the most encouraging things in the movement is the army of younger leaders from close to a hundred nationalities that God has raised up to carry the vision and the work forward.

My own life and the lives of Drena and our small staff have also become more complex. We seem to have less time to do things we used to do. We have discovered a whole series of different obstacles as we walk down this road, but in the end we are cast on God as we have always been. We have seen amazing answers to prayer, and thanks to some great books we know more about how to handle unanswered prayer. If you are challenged by this in your life, I recommend *God on Mute: Engaging the Silence of Unanswered Prayer* by Pete Greig, the founder of the 24-7 prayer movement.

Chapter 14

A BURDEN AND VISION THAT HAS NEVER CHANGED

I had a love for the Bible even before my conversion. Both receiving a gospel of John in the mail during the summer of 1953 and hearing Billy Graham on March 3, 1955, changed the course of my life. Even before that I attended the Bible Club at Ramsey High School, which was probably the reason I got the following letter together with the gospel of John:

MESSIOLOGY

Word of Life Camp
Schroon Lake, New York
July 15, 1953

Dear Bible Club Member:

The summer is well started now, and I hope that you are truly enjoying it. Whether you are working or resting, I imagine that you have some spare time. As Bible Club president, I have always desired that each member read at least a portion of the Bible. During the school year, our time is quite occupied with school work, but now that you have a little time, I would like to invite you to read the portion of God's Word which is enclosed, the Gospel of John.

There are several reasons, which I shall briefly state, why I would like you to read it. First of all the Bible itself tells you to "Search the Scriptures" in John 5:39. This is one of God's commands which we should obey. Also, there are many interesting stories in the Bible of miracles and exciting experiences which are all true, as it says in John 17:17 -- "Thy word is truth." Also, the Bible has been a great source of enjoyment and blessing to many, including me. Only in this Book do we find God's instructions for us and our lives.

The time spent in reading this short book would be most worthwhile and inspiriting. In this short portion are included most of the basic Bible truths, and the way to find true joy, peace, and success.

This summer will be only as worthwhile as the things which you do in it. Reading this short portion of God's Word will be very worthwhile, and I pray that it may be the source of joy and blessing. If you have any questions or problems in which I might help, please let me know. I would be most happy to help you.

God bless you in His path.

Yours most truly,

Dannie

Daniel Clapp

I also joined the Pocket Testament League around that same time and carried a New Testament in my pocket. I saw one of their presentations that showed their gospel preaching and distribution of John's gospel. So the seed of wanting everyone in the world to have the Word of God was sown in my heart.

Most people know I am involved in many aspects of God's work and also know how much I esteem all agencies and churches that are part of God's great global force. What I share below comes from my heart with a lot of thought from a lifetime of ministry.

On my last trip to India I did some homework and interviewed many people and realized that, despite all the fantastic ministries—including mass evangelism, radio, TV, film shows, and literature—there are still hundreds of millions who have never heard the gospel in any form. Also, many groups have moved into holistic ministry, like the schools we have among the Dalits, which involves a significant amount of time and money. Tremendous evangelism and church planting is done side-by-side and we thank the Lord for results.

However, though the Dalits may soon be the most reached group in India, with around 250 million people, what percentage of them will we actually reach knowing that many of them do not read? We are told there are somewhere around

300 million "Other Backward Castes" (OBC), maybe more, and I wonder how many have not yet had one chance to hear of or know the saving grace of Christ? This is from someone who believes that one chance to hear of Jesus is not enough.

There are over 170 million Muslims in India. Maybe if we are optimistic, many millions have been to a gospel film show or have a New Testament or gospel or may have heard or seen a gospel radio or TV program. What if it were even 70 million? That's 100 million to go! Do you get my point? I am not up-to-date on China, but with all the growth there no one would question that hundreds of millions have never heard.

I recently noticed huge steps forward to get the Bible or parts of it in every language. It's great to read that many millions of dollars are now given or pledged to this. But this makes it more difficult for me to understand how there are hundreds of millions (some would say a billion) all around us in whose languages we have already translated gospel materials, and yet we still have not given anything to them. This doesn't make sense!

One group claims that we will soon lead another billion to Christ. I believe this is misleading, but with certain parts of the world having massive church growth, who knows? The truth is that we'll only have a small effect on the hundreds of millions who are more resistant to the gospel or live away from the areas where this response is taking place. For example, will Dalit converts in India reach Brahmans?

My plea is that we would pray more for the reaching of these unreached hundreds of millions with the message of salvation. Would you pray for the release of funds for this kind of ministry? Financial breakthroughs will enable us to give more evangelistic tools to thousands of workers who are asking for them. It will not be one agency or church that makes this happen, but a massive grassroots movement (already going on) in which people even in the midst of other ministry want to reach the millions around them. We need to make every effort to teach each believer in every new church that they should be reaching out to all the lost around them. This would be a gigantic step forward.

A few years ago I decided to make a list of those ministries that have given the gospel to at least 100 million. I called it "The Hundred Million Club." I have a list of about fifty agencies and ministries. Of course, many people in certain nations and language groups have read the gospel many times. Some have a pile of gospels. And yet, hundreds of millions still have nothing. We have much to rejoice over, but we also have so much to do.

I hope you will become part of the vision and action.

Chapter 15

FROM YOUR HEAD TO YOUR HEART TO YOUR FEET

I am here in the beautiful home of dear friends outside one of my favorite cities, Belfast, Northern Ireland. I have been here about a hundred times, counting visits to other parts of Ireland, and it's amazing to see all that God is doing in the midst of what for decades was one of the biggest and most horrific messes in all of Europe.

All these years I have listened to criticism of the churches for not doing more about it. How easy it is to blame the church! If the church was so bad then why was the living God using the church here and saving so many people in the midst of all this? It is one of the first places in the world that gave me a wide open door to speak at one of their biggest and most important missions events. It became the most proactive part of the UK, for not only OM but dozens of other missions groups. How could God ever use a church that holds such prejudice against the Catholic population? This sad division exists to this day and I find it a great struggle . . . but the Living God seems to be able to handle it. God Almighty can be grieved by people and bless people at the same time. Yes, as you are now understanding, this is what I call *messiology*.

This is my final chapter and my heart and mind are so full of what I would like to share. You may wonder why there is not more about missions and especially the unreached people in this book, but I did not want to repeat what I have written about in my other books. There is also the official history of OM called *Spiritual Revolution* by Ian Randall, which expresses so much of what I believe and how God has worked in my life and in OM. There also are quite a number of books about the ship ministry, including unique books like Deborah Meroff's *Psalms from the Sea*.

I want to give a final plea for you to consider becoming a career missionary. Some don't like the word missionary, so what about a full-time ambassador of Christ to the nations? This is the decision Drena and I made before we even met, and we now look back at fifty-five years of work and service together. Even at this point in her life Drena is a full-time missionary working very long hours every day behind the scenes. We don't believe in retirement in our service for the King. I already have a strategy for how I can stay in bed with my smartphone and laptop and carry on a good part of my work, should that become necessary.

How sad that so many churches now have ignored Acts 13 and no longer send out long-term career missionaries from their church. This includes good churches that I highly esteem. I am well aware of some of the negative stories circulated about missionaries (some of which are true) that cause even well-known Christian leaders to develop false ideas. Even so, do we have any idea of how many millions upon millions have come to Christ and are still coming to Christ because we have sent out missionaries? Some of those places don't need so many anymore but there are other nations, at least forty, that desperately need long-term, language-learning missionaries. I believe also in tentmakers who have a job or business for income in addition to vocational ministry but, so often in my observation, their work becomes all-consuming, especially if they have a family, and there is little time left for sharing the gospel and planting a church. We rejoice over every exception.

OM has been considered one of the major organizations birthing short-term missions but that was not my original intent. From day one we have been looking for "lifers."

We saw right away in Mexico and much more in Europe how wonderfully God could use short-term missions, which in turn became a global phenomenon bringing hundreds of thousands into the kingdom. Yes, there were lots of mistakes along the way and it's been very messy. But also worth it.

In all of this we learned that so often the finances were harder to find than the people. We saw great answers to prayer in connection with funds and OM was considered part of the Faith Mission Movement, which was pioneered without them knowing it by people like Hudson Taylor, C. T. Studd, and many others.

George Mueller, for instance, did not outwardly ask for money, but moved his whole work mainly among orphans by faith and prayer. In the culture of his day George was a fantastic fundraiser and I decided to follow his example. Praying and finding the finance for OM and other ministries has been one of the most exciting and motivating parts of my life. The New Testament clearly shows that together with prayer we need the highest level of communication, openness, honesty, and integrity. The latest book to help me on this subject is called *Gospel Patrons* by John Rinehart. He shares about how the business people, who have the gift and ability to make money, are so often such a vital part of what God is doing through other anointed and gifted people.

If the message of grace, mystery, and mercy has not emanated from these pages, then I have failed. Some of you who are reading this have not yet received God's gift of salvation by believing on the Lord Jesus that He died for your sins. You need to do that now.

Others who have had this experience of new birth and grace have not forgiven themselves. This brings ongoing dysfunction and complexity in their lives and ministry. We surely have seen that God not only works in messy situations that must grieve Him, but He can work in messy people. He wants to use you no matter how many struggles and failures you have had in your life! Maybe, due to sin and folly, you walk with a limp—but you're still walking! He may want you walking in some other part of the world where you never expected to go. Would you at least pray about it?

Some who are reading this have not really forgiven others, especially those who have hurt, disappointed, or even betrayed them. Maybe they have forgiven them in theory but not in practice. It might be an ongoing struggle, but that step needs to be taken.

If God has spoken to you through what I have shared,

I would like you to consider some other practical steps to move this message from your head down to your heart and then your feet!

Make the decision to be more positive and optimistic. Start by sharing some of the wonderful ways God is working locally and around the world.

Get involved in at least one prayer group of some kind that focuses on the nations and unreached peoples. Hopefully you're involved in your local church prayer meeting but I would hope you can be involved in at least one other one. Or maybe just start one!

Get involved in giving out books and resources that have helped you, and especially those that include portions of Scripture. Give them to those you know or meet who don't know the Lord. It should be obvious by now from all the books I've mentioned that this is one of my favorite things to do!

Go on a short-term mission trip ASAP. Try to give preference to a ministry where you will be sharing your faith and involved with people. Try to work among the poor and live in a situation where you will be stretched.

Go out of your way to meet people near you from other cultures. Start learning another language. If you have already studied a language, as I started Spanish in high school, then make a decision to continue to become fluent. Get among people who have this as their first language. *Choose the difficult road on purpose.*

Practice using your time more productively. "Less watching others act and more acting myself" should be our motto. Beware of the television trap, game trap, and chit-chat trap. There is room for all of these things and much more—but they should not be our priority or focus. Of course if you have children and grandchildren then that time has to increase. Also with friends who are not believers, we must remember Paul's words in 1 Corinthians 9:22, *To the weak I became weak, to win the weak. I have become all things to all people so that by all possible means I might save some.*

Give thought to going to Bible college. This can even be done by distance learning or extension. We have an over fifty-three-year relationship with Capernwray Fellowship, which has short-term Bible schools in different parts of the world. One way or another, you need more time in the Word of God. I especially urge people to memorize Scripture, which has helped transform my own life even before my conversion.

Make the decision to practice being more thankful every day. Has anyone given you anything lately? Even a book, a cup of tea, or a ride to the station? Have you thanked them? I thank Jesus that He has forgiven me for the times I have not been thankful or thanked people properly with love.

Work harder at getting a good amount of exercise and sleep, and eating the right food. This has been my lifelong practice and I really recommend it. One of the most powerful passages in the New Testament for me is 1 Corinthians 9:24–27:

> *Do you not know that in a race all the runners run, but only one gets the prize? Run in such a way as to get the prize. Everyone who competes in the games goes into strict training. They do it to get a crown that will not last, but we do it to get a crown that will last forever. Therefore I do not run like someone running aimlessly; I do not fight like a boxer beating the air. No, I strike a blow to my body and make it my slave so that after I have preached to others, I myself will not be disqualified for the prize.*

Make a decision to be in touch with more people. Use a good variety of methods but remember face-to-face over a coffee or tea is the best. Going out together loving, serving, and reaching others might be even better. This must be mixed with forgiveness as people may let you down or you might feel some rejection in it all. The great mistake is to fail to take the initiative. I am in touch with many people who need money and I have a fund for just such people, but guess why so many never get any money? They never ask! By the way, there are fantastic books on how to raise funds like *Funding the Family Business* by Myles Wilson and *Friend Raising* by Betty Barnett.

Try to get some kind of mentoring and accountability even if it seems imperfect. If you are married, make sure you are getting enough time with your spouse and family. Don't expect it to be easy. As you've heard me say throughout this book, there's a degree of messiness in all things. And yet, thanks to God's sovereignty and grace, He takes our weakness and transforms it into His glory.

For me, finishing this book has been a long marathon, but I see the finishing tape ahead and I am thankful for all the help from Above along the way. I am also thankful for all the wonderful people of God who have influenced my life these seventy-six years, and I humble myself before the Lord in thanksgiving and worship.

I am hoping that some who read this book will join with us in this great vision and task. Feel free to contact me at george.verwer@om.org. I answer every email personally!

God bless you.